BuzzPop

An imprint of Bonnier Publishing USA
251 Park Avenue South, New York, NY 10010
Text copyright © 2019 by Bonnier Publishing USA
Illustrations copyright © 2019 by Kyle Beckett
BuzzPop is a trademark of Bonnier Publishing USA, and
associated colophon is a trademark of Bonnier Publishing USA.
Manufactured in the United States of America
First Edition
10 9 8 7 6 5 4 3 2 1
ISBN 978-1-4998-0948-0
buzzpopbooks.com
bonnierpublishingusa.com

Ten little monkeys jumping on the bed,
one jumped up and bumped his head.

Mother called the doctor and the doctor said, "No more monkeys jumping on the bed."

Nine little monkeys jumping on the bed,
one jumped up and bumped her head.

Mother called the doctor and the doctor said, "No more monkeys jumping on the bed."

Eight little monkeys jumping on the bed,
one jumped up and bumped his head.

Mother called the doctor and the doctor said, "No more monkeys jumping on the bed."

Seven little monkeys jumping on the bed,
one jumped up and bumped his head.

Mother called the doctor and the doctor said, "No more monkeys jumping on the bed."

Six little monkeys jumping on the bed,
one jumped up and bumped his head.

Mother called the doctor and the doctor said, "No more monkeys jumping on the bed."

Five little monkeys jumping on the bed,
one jumped up and bumped his head.

Mother called the doctor and the doctor said, "No more monkeys jumping on the bed."

Four little monkeys jumping on the bed,
one jumped up and bumped his head.

Mother called the doctor
and the doctor said,
"No more monkeys
jumping on the bed."

Three little monkeys jumping on the bed,
one jumped up and bumped his head.

Mother called the doctor
and the doctor said,
"No more monkeys
jumping on the bed."

Two little monkeys jumping on the bed,
one jumped up and bumped her head.

Mother called the doctor and the doctor said, "No more monkeys jumping on the bed."

One little monkey jumping on the bed,
he jumped up and bumped his head.

Mother called the doctor and the doctor said,
"No more monkeys jumping on the bed!"

Who's Who?

Michael Flynn (National Security Advisor, Jan. 20–Feb. 13, 2017)—As Director of the Defense Intelligence Agency, Lt. General Michael Flynn served under Obama for two years. As Trump's National Security Advisor, though, Flynn served just over three weeks. He was fired for misrepresenting the extent of his communications with Russian Ambassador Sergey Kaslyek, and was most recently reported to have made a deal with Special Prosecutor Robert Mueller, who is investigating the possibility of Trump's collusion with Russia during the 2016 election.

Katie Walsh (White House Deputy Chief of Staff, Jan. 20–Mar. 30, 2017)—Walsh rose up through the ranks of the Republican National Committee to serve as Chief of Staff under Reince Priebus, and joined the Trump transition team. Reporting to Priebus again as the Deputy Chief of Staff, Walsh lasted just over two months before transitioning out of the Trump administrative staff and into America First Policies, a nonprofit suspected to be a "dark money" super PAC for Republicans.

Michael Dubke (White House Communications Director, Mar. 6–Jun. 2, 2017)—A veteran of political media relations and strategy, Mike Dubke seemed credibly qualified to step into the role of Communications Director during a time when Press Secretary Sean Spicer's relationship with the press was considered contentious. Dubke came in and left three months later, citing "personal reasons" for his resignation.

Sean Spicer (White House Press Secretary, Jan. 20–Jul. 21, 2017)—As Trump's first Press Secretary, Sean Spicer set the tone for the administration's adversarial relationship with the media. His statements were recast as "alternative facts" by a defensive White House, as opposed to "inaccurate" or "outright lies." The constant queries about leaks from White House staff to the press, and Spicer's natural charisma caused Trump to appoint Dubke as Communications Director over Spicer. When Dubke departed, however, Spicer took over as Communications Director until Anthony Scaramucci arrived.

Reince Priebus (White House Chief of Staff, Jan. 20–Jul. 31, 2017)—As chairman of the Republican National Committee, Reince Priebus was a strong influence on both the GOP platform and its candidates. During the election, Priebus supported Trump's candidacy despite several disagreements with Trump on strategy. In return, Priebus was made White House Chief of Staff. His six-month tenure won him no friends among the president's chief advisors, and his resignation was handed in after Anthony Scaramucci insinuated that Priebus was guilty of leaking information to the media.

Anthony Scaramucci (White House Communications Director, Jul. 21–31, 2017)—More of an opportunist than a conservative, Anthony Scaramucci blew into town promising a smoother relationship with the press than was enjoyed by Sean Spicer. He then destroyed any credibility whatsoever during an interview with the *New Yorker* wherein he was a little too frank and seemingly unaware of being on record. During his remarkable ten-day tenure, the "Mooch" insulted advisor Steve Bannon, inferred Reince Priebus was to blame for the leaks, and exited nearly as quickly as he arrived, resigning to new Chief of Staff John Kelly.

Steve Bannon (White House Chief Strategist and Counselor to the President, Jan. 20–Aug. 18, 2017)—As cofounder of alt-right opinion site Breitbart, Bannon's credentials for a government position seemed shaky. His duties were equally mysterious. Bannon briefly enjoyed an appointment to the National Security Council before being removed by Michael Flynn's replacement, H. R. McMaster. Bannon returned the favor by allegedly leaking unflattering information about McMaster to right-wing pundits. During the Unite the Right march build-up and its aftermath, Bannon finally made his exit from the White House, but not before imploring Trump to condemn "both sides" for the Charlottesville tragedy.

Tom Price (Secretary of Health and Human Services, Feb. 10–Sept. 29, 2017)—As a lifelong politician, Tom Price was one of Trump's more qualified appointments. Undoubtedly taking his cues from the president, Price saw nothing wrong with constantly using private charter jets and military aircraft for his personal travel. However, the taxpayers footing the bill certainly minded, and even Price's fellow Republicans questioned the appropriateness of Price's travel arrangements. Price resigned after nearly ten months at his position, making his tenure the shortest in history for the HHS Secretary post.

Brenda Fitzgerald (Director of the Centers for Disease Control and Prevention, Jul. 7, 2017–Jan. 31, 2018)—Appointed to her position by Tom Price, Brenda Fitzgerald failed to take into account how her financial stakes in both a Japanese tobacco company and prescription drug monitoring programs might conflict with her role. Forcefully reminded of this potential conflict of interest thanks to a report from Politico, Fitzgerald resigned her post the day after their article ran.

Rex Tillerson (Secretary of State, Feb. 1, 2017–Mar. 31, 2018)—A Texas oil businessman is naturally a diplomat, so who better to lead the State Department, right? Tillerson's tenure saw a massive reorganization of the diplomatic ranks, an action which has been continually referred to as a total disaster. Although Tillerson held onto his position for over a year, his increasingly divergent approach from Trump's methods led the secretary to refer to the president as a "moron." Trump, with his usual grace, fired Tillerson, awarding him the dubious honor of being the first Secretary of State to have been openly canned since 1945.